conte

British & North American Readers:
Please note that Australian cup and spoon measurements are metric. A quick conversion guide appears on page 63. A glossary explaining unfamiliar terms and ingredients begins on page 60.

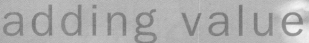

adding value

*One of the nicest ways to give a gift of food
is to place it in a lovely container that
is itself a gift. Fill a cup or mug with
homemade cookies, or give a lovely
glass jar filled with herbed vinegar.
You can also use commercial biscuit tins —
line them first with crisp baking paper.
It will give your gift a fresh, clean look, and
help to keep the biscuits or cakes fresh.*

4 chilli and lemon grass
flavoured olives

Give these as part of a Mediterranean hamper with Tomato Caper Tapenade, Fetta Cheese in Herb Oil and Italian Dried Capsicums. Include some fresh crusty bread.

1 lime

600g black olives, drained

1¹/₂ teaspoons cumin seeds

¹/₄ cup chopped fresh lemon grass

1 baby (25g) white onion, chopped finely

2 small fresh red chillies, chopped finely

3 cups (750ml) hot olive oil, approximately

Using a vegetable peeler, peel rind from lime; cut rind into fine strips. Combine rind, olives, seeds, lemon grass, onion and chilli in bowl.

Place olive mixture into hot sterilised 1-litre (4-cup) jar; pour in enough hot oil (taking care as it will bubble) to cover olives completely, leaving 1cm space between oil and top of jar; seal immediately.

Best made 1 week ahead
Storage refrigerator, up to 2 months

tomato caper
tapenade

Give tapendade along with some good bread: a loaf of rye, a fancy wholemeal loaf or some homemade pitta crisps.

³/₄ cup (110g) sun-dried tomatoes in oil, drained, chopped

¹/₄ cup (60ml) olive oil

¹/₄ cup (45g) drained capers

2 cloves garlic, chopped

1 teaspoon grated lemon rind

1 tablespoon lemon juice

1 tablespoon fresh thyme leaves

Process all ingredients until smooth.
Spoon into hot sterilised jar; seal immediately.

Makes about 1 cup (250ml)
Best made 1 day ahead
Storage refrigerator, up to 6 weeks

fetta cheese in herb oil

Serving suggestions for the label: scatter on salads, especially those made from baby spinach or mixed salad leaves, melt on top of a homemade pizza, or serve as part of an antipasto or cheese platter.

500g block fetta cheese

1¹/₂ cups (375ml) milk

1¹/₂ cups (375ml) water

3 sprigs fresh thyme

2 sprigs fresh rosemary

4 bay leaves

3 small fresh red chillies

1 tablespoon yellow mustard seeds

2 teaspoons fennel seeds

2 teaspoons dried juniper berries

1 teaspoon grated lemon rind

2 cups (500ml) olive oil, approximately

Cut cheese into 3cm slices, place in large bowl; pour over milk and water; cover, refrigerate overnight. Drain cheese; discard milk mixture. Place cheese, herbs, chillies, seeds, berries and rind in large jar; cover with oil, leaving 1cm space between oil and top of jar; seal jar.

Best made 1 day ahead
Storage cool, dark place, up to 2 weeks

laksa paste

This can be beautifully presented in a bamboo steamer basket with some packaged dried noodles; tie some fresh lemon grass and dried chillies into the gift ribbon in place of a bow.

2 teaspoons blacan

1 large (200g) brown onion, chopped

4 cloves garlic, chopped

1 teaspoon grated lime rind

1 teaspoon ground turmeric

1 tablespoon chopped fresh lemon grass

1 tablespoon grated fresh ginger

1 tablespoon roughly chopped Vietnamese mint

3 small fresh red chillies

8 (20g) candlenuts

2 teaspoons ground coriander

2 tablespoons roughly chopped fresh coriander (including roots)

3/4 cup (180ml) vegetable oil

Cook blacan in small non-stick pan until fragrant. Blend or process blacan, onion, garlic, rind, turmeric, lemon grass, ginger, mint, chillies, candlenuts, ground coriander, fresh coriander and 1/2 cup of the oil until mixture forms a paste.

Spoon into hot sterilised jars, add remaining oil, leaving 1cm space between oil and top of jar; seal jar.

Makes about 1 cup (250ml)
Best made 1 day ahead
Storage refrigerator, up to 1 month

8 spicy mixed nuts

Nuts and boutique beer make a fine Father's Day present.

2 tablespoons vegetable oil

1 cup (150g) raw peanuts

1 cup (150g) raw cashews

1 cup (150g) shelled pistachios

1 cup (160g) blanched almonds

2 teaspoons garam masala

1 teaspoon salt

Heat oil in pan; cook the peanuts, stirring until browned lightly; drain on absorbent paper. Repeat process with cashews and remaining nuts.

Cook garam masala in same pan, stirring until fragrant. Combine garam masala with nuts and salt in large bowl; cool. Store in airtight containers.

Makes about 4 cups
Best made 1 day ahead
Storage airtight container, up to 2 weeks

plum and port sauce

This sauce is delicious with beef, pork or game; a copy of your favourite roast beef, pork or game recipe would make this gift complete.

1 tablespoon olive oil

2 medium (300g) brown onions, chopped

3 cloves garlic, crushed

1/4 cup (60ml) red wine vinegar

1/4 cup (50g) brown sugar

1/4 teaspoon salt

8 medium (1.5kg) tomatoes, peeled, chopped

6 medium (780g) blood plums, peeled, seeded, chopped

1 cup (250ml) port

2 teaspoons juniper berries

Makes about 1 litre (4 cups)
Best made 1 day ahead
Storage refrigerator, about 2 weeks

Heat oil in large pan, add onion and garlic, cook, stirring, until onion is soft. Add remaining ingredients, stir over heat, without boiling, until sugar is dissolved. Simmer, uncovered, stirring occasionally, about 30 minutes or until sauce has thickened.

Blend or process mixture in batches until finely chopped; strain, discard pulp. Pour hot sauce into hot sterilised bottles; seal immediately.

10 red curry paste

Give this paste to known curry-lovers and include a recipe for a curry that uses it.

6 dried red chillies, seeded, chopped

2 medium (300g) brown onions, chopped

3 cloves garlic, crushed

2 tablespoons peanut oil

1 teaspoon grated lemon rind

2 teaspoons shrimp paste

1 tablespoon ground cumin

1 tablespoon mild sweet paprika

2 teaspoons ground turmeric

1 teaspoon ground black pepper

Blend or process all ingredients until thick and smooth. Spoon into hot sterilised jars; seal immediately.

Makes about 1 cup (250ml)
Best made 1 day ahead
Storage refrigerator, up to 1 month

green masala paste

Make a curry-lover's dream come true, give this curry paste along with Red Curry Paste and Chilli Jam. Expect some great dinner invitations.

2 teaspoons fenugreek seeds

2 tablespoons grated fresh ginger

1 teaspoon ground turmeric

3/4 teaspoon ground cloves

3 cloves garlic, chopped

11/4 cups firmly packed fresh coriander leaves

1 cup firmly packed fresh mint leaves

11/2 teaspoons ground cardamom

1/2 cup (125ml) brown vinegar

1/4 cup (60ml) peanut oil

1 tablespoon sesame oil

Place seeds in small bowl, cover with boiling water, stand 10 minutes; drain. Blend or process seeds, ginger, turmeric, cloves, garlic, coriander, mint, cardamom and vinegar until combined.

Heat oils in medium pan, stir in herb-spice mixture. Bring to boil, remove from heat. Pour into hot sterilised jars; seal immediately.

Makes about 1 cup (250ml)
Best made 1 day ahead
Storage refrigerator, up to 1 month

12 rich blue cheese and poppyseed biscuits

Wrap up these delicious biscuits with a wedge of strong blue cheese for a perfect gift.

Process flour, butter and cheese until mixture forms a soft ball. Place mixture on plastic wrap and shape into a log 4cm in diameter, refrigerate until firm.

Remove log from plastic, roll in seeds, cut into 5mm slices. Place rounds about 3cm apart on ungreased oven trays, sprinkle with a little salt. Bake in moderately hot oven about 15 minutes or until lightly browned; cool on trays.

1 cup (150g) plain flour
100g cold butter, chopped
75g mild full-fat soft blue cheese, chopped
1¹/₂ tablespoons poppyseeds
sea salt

Makes about 30
Best made 1 day ahead
Storage airtight container, up to 5 days

pizza-flavoured
crisps

This recipe makes a crisp suitable for all kinds of vegetable dips — give the dip as well (or the recipe), and a bottle of red wine.

Add flours to large bowl, rub in butter, stir in cheese, olives, paste, bacon, basil, yolk and enough water to mix to a soft dough. Knead dough on lightly floured surface until smooth.

Divide dough into 3 portions, roll each portion between sheets of baking paper to a 27 x 32cm rectangle. Place each rectangle onto a greased oven tray. Bake in moderately hot oven about 15 minutes or until browned.

Turn rectangle over, bake further 5 minutes or until browned underneath. Cool on wire racks; break into large pieces to serve.

Best made 1 day ahead
Storage airtight container, up to 5 days

1/2 cup (75g) plain flour

1 1/2 cups (225g) self-raising flour

90g butter, chopped

1/2 cup (40g) grated parmesan cheese

1/2 cup (60g) seeded black olives, chopped finely

1/4 cup (60ml) tomato paste

3 bacon rashers, chopped finely

2 tablespoons chopped fresh basil

1 egg yolk

1 tablespoon water, approximately

14 citrus duck pate

with seed crackers

Give pate and crackers together or separately. If you are feeling lavish you could present them in a basket with a pate knife.

500g duck livers

1/3 cup (80ml) dry vermouth

125g butter

6 green onions, chopped

1 clove garlic, crushed

2 teaspoons chopped fresh rosemary

2 teaspoons chopped fresh thyme

1/2 cup (125ml) cream

2 tablespoons orange-flavoured liqueur

1 teaspoon grated orange rind

125g butter, melted, extra

2 fresh bay leaves

seed crackers

1 cup (150g) plain flour

30g butter

1 tablespoon poppyseeds

1 tablespoon sesame seeds

1 egg, beaten lightly

1 tablespoon water

2 teaspoons milk

1 tablespoon sea salt

Clean livers, discard fat. Place livers and vermouth in bowl, cover, refrigerate 2 hours. **Heat** half the butter in a pan, add onion, garlic and herbs, cook until onion is soft. Stir in undrained livers, cook about 5 minutes or until livers are just cooked. Drain livers, reserving liquid. Melt remaining butter. **Blend** or process liver mixture, and, with motor operating, gradually add 1/2 cup (125ml) reserved liquid in a thin stream with the melted butter. Add cream, liqueur and rind, process until smooth. Push mixture through sieve into two 2-cup (500ml) capacity bowls; cover, refrigerate 2 hours. **Heat** extra butter in a pan. Pour over pate, discarding milky residue. Decorate tops with bay leaves. Serve with Seed Crackers. **Seed Crackers** Place flour in medium bowl, rub in butter, stir in seeds. Add egg and enough water to make ingredients cling together. Knead on floured surface, until smooth. Divide dough into quarters, roll each portion to 1mm thick. Place on lightly oiled oven trays, brush with milk, sprinkle with salt. **Bake** in moderate oven 10 minutes or until well browned. Cool on rack.

Makes about 1 litre (4 cups) pate

Best made 1 day ahead

Storage pate, refrigerator, up to 3 days; seed crackers, airtight container, up to 1 week

fresh tomato
pasta sauce

To make this into a special gift add a packet of fancy pasta, a wedge of parmesan cheese and a jar of beautiful black olives.

2 tablespoons olive oil

1 large (200g) brown onion, chopped

2 cloves garlic, crushed

10 medium (2kg) tomatoes, peeled, chopped

2 teaspoons salt

1/2 cup (125ml) dry red wine

2 teaspoons brown sugar

2 tablespoons tomato paste

2 tablespoons finely chopped fresh basil leaves

2 tablespoons finely chopped fresh parsley

2 teaspoons finely chopped fresh oregano

1/2 teaspoon cracked black peppercorns

Heat oil in large pan, cook onion and garlic, stirring, until onion is soft. Add tomatoes, salt and wine, simmer, uncovered, about 15 minutes or until tomatoes are soft.

Add remaining ingredients, simmer, uncovered, about 10 minutes or until thickened. Pour sauce into hot sterilised bottles; seal immediately.

Makes about 1.75 litres (7 cups)
Best made 1 day ahead
Storage refrigerator, up to 1 week or freeze, in plastic containers, up to 2 months

italian

dried capsicums

Give a jar of these delicious capsicums with a loaf of sourdough bread and a hunk of vintage cheese.

2kg red or green capsicums, quartered

4 cloves garlic, peeled

2 teaspoons dried rosemary

2 teaspoons dried tarragon

olive oil

Place capsicums, cut-side down on wire rack. Cook in very slow oven, 3 hours. Add garlic to capsicums, cook further 1 hour or until capsicums are dry. Turn and rearrange capsicums during drying process.
Pack capsicums into hot sterilised jars with garlic and herbs, pour enough oil over capsicums to cover completely; seal jars.

Best made 1 week ahead
Storage refrigerator, up to 2 months

flavoured
vinegars

These vinegars, along with a bottle of extra-virgin olive oil and a simple salad dressing recipe, make a perfect summer gift.

herb and garlic vinegar

1 litre (4 cups) white wine vinegar

8 sprigs fresh tarragon

2 cloves garlic, peeled, sliced

peppered rosemary vinegar

1 litre (4 cups) red wine vinegar

10 black peppercorns

10 sprigs fresh rosemary

berry cardamom vinegar

1 litre (4 cups) white wine vinegar

300g raspberries

10 cardamom pods, crushed

Wash fresh herbs or berries and pat dry before using. Combine all the ingredients for your chosen vinegar in large jug or bowl; cover tightly and refrigerate for 3 days. Pour the vinegar (strained if you wish) into dry sterilised bottles; seal tightly. **Fresh** herbs can be added just before giving away the vinegars, but they too will discolour with time.

Makes about 1 litre (4 cups) each vinegar
Best made 1 week ahead
Storage cool dark place, up to 3 months

pesto

A jar of homemade pesto, a chunk of fresh parmesan and a packet of good durum wheat pasta: what more could one want?

4 cups firmly packed fresh basil leaves

1 cup (160g) pine nuts, toasted

4 cloves garlic, chopped

1 cup (250ml) olive oil

2/3 cup (50g) grated parmesan cheese

extra olive oil

Process basil, nuts and garlic until finely chopped. Add oil in thin stream while motor is operating, process until combined. Add cheese, process until mixture is combined. Spoon into hot sterilised jars; drizzle a thin layer of extra oil over top to cover pesto, leaving 1cm space between oil and top of jars; seal jars.

Makes about 2¹/₂ cups
Best made 1 day ahead
Storage refrigerator, up to 2 weeks

oat biscuits

Wrap these up with some crumbly vintage cheddar.

Process oats until finely ground. Place flour in large bowl with oats and sugar; rub in butter. Combine golden syrup and milk in small pan, stir over heat until warm. Stir warm milk mixture into oat mixture, mix to a soft dough; knead gently on lightly floured surface until smooth.

Roll dough between sheets of baking paper until 3mm thick; cut unto 6cm rounds, place about 2cm apart on greased oven trays; prick all over with fork. Bake in moderate oven about 12 minutes or until lightly browned; cool on trays.

Makes about 35
Best made 1 day ahead
Storage airtight container, up to 5 days

3 cups (270g) rolled oats
1 cup (160g) wholemeal plain flour
1/3 cup (65g) firmly packed brown sugar
60g butter, chopped
1/4 cup (60ml) golden syrup
1/3 cup (80ml) milk

bottled
antipasto

You can give lots of things with this antipasto to make it a special gift: cheese, olives, breadsticks, crackers, salami, or you can just wrap some raffia around the neck of the jar of antipasto.

2 medium (400g) red capsicums
1 medium (300g) yellow capsicum
3 medium (360g) zucchini
4 (240g) finger eggplants
4 large (1kg) tomatoes
1 tablespoon dried thyme leaves

1 tablespoon fine sea salt
1 teaspoon ground black pepper
1/2 cup (125ml) vegetable oil
1 1/4 cups (310ml) olive oil
2 tablespoons balsamic vinegar

Quarter capsicums, remove seeds and membranes. Grill capsicum, skin-side up, until skin blisters and blackens. Peel away skin, slice capsicum thickly. Cut zucchini and eggplants lengthways into 5mm slices, cut in half. Trim tomatoes at both ends, cut in half.

Cook zucchini and eggplants in batches on heated greased griddle pan until browned and tender. Cook tomatoes in batches on same pan, until browned and just tender. Pack hot vegetables into a wide-necked, hot sterilised jar (1.5-litre/6-cup capacity).

Combine thyme, salt, pepper and oils in small pan, stir over heat until hot. Remove from heat, carefully add vinegar, the mixture will bubble fiercely. Pour enough oil mixture into jar to cover vegetable mixture completely, leaving a 1cm space between the lid and oil; seal immediately.

Best made 1 day ahead
Storage refrigerator, up to 2 weeks

chilli jam

Chilli Jam and the two curry pastes, Red Curry Paste and Green Masala Paste, will make most curry-lovers happy.

4 medium (760g) tomatoes, chopped

1 tablespoon Worcestershire sauce

1/2 cup (125ml) sweet chilli sauce

1/3 cup (80ml) water

1/3 cup (75g) firmly packed brown sugar

1 tablespoon chopped fresh coriander leaves

Combine tomatoes, sauces, water, and sugar in medium pan; stir over heat until sugar dissolves. Bring to boil, simmer, uncovered, 45 minutes or until jam thickens and is reduced to about 1 1/3 cups (330ml). Stir constantly towards end of cooking time to prevent mixture from burning.
Remove from heat; stand 10 minutes, add coriander. Spoon into hot sterilised jars; seal immediately.
Makes about 1 1/3 cups (330ml)
Best made 1 day ahead
Storage refrigerator, up to 1 month

harissa

This North African recipe is great as a marinade for grilled chicken, fish or lamb. Wear rubber gloves when handling chillies — they can irritate the skin, especially when you're dealing with large quantities of chillies.

100g dried red chillies, seeded, chopped

3 cloves garlic, crushed

1/2 teaspoon salt

3 teaspoons coriander seeds

3 teaspoons cumin seeds

1 1/2 teaspoons caraway seeds

2 teaspoons dried mint leaves

1/2 cup (125ml) olive oil

Place chillies in bowl; cover with hot water; stand 20 minutes. Drain chillies; discard water. Process chillies, garlic, salt, seeds and mint until smooth. Reserve 1 tablespoon oil. Add remaining oil to chilli mixture, in thin stream, while motor is operating; process until combined.

Spoon harissa into hot sterilised jars, drizzle with reserved oil to cover, leaving 1cm space between oil and top of jar; seal.

Makes about 1 1/2 cups
Best made 2 days ahead
Storage refrigerator, up to 6 weeks

oregano
breadsticks

Give Oregano Breadsticks and Bottled Antipasto to a picnic-loving friend, or take them along as your contribution to the picnic.

50g butter, melted

1 teaspoon dried yeast

2 tablespoons olive oil

2 teaspoons sugar

1/2 teaspoon salt

1 tablespoon dried oregano leaves

1 cup (80g) grated parmesan cheese

3/4 cup (180ml) water

2 1/2 cups (375g) plain flour

Combine butter, yeast, oil, sugar, salt, oregano, cheese and water in large bowl; gradually stir in flour.
Knead on lightly floured surface until smooth and elastic (about 10 minutes). Place dough in large oiled bowl; cover with plastic wrap. Stand dough in warm place for 10 minutes.
Cut dough into quarters. Roll each quarter into 10 logs about 20cm long. Place on lightly greased oven trays.
Bake in hot oven for about 20 minutes or until crisp and browned. Place on wire racks to cool.

Makes 40
Best made 1 day ahead
Storage airtight container, up to 2 weeks

peach relish

Peach Relish makes a great accompaniment to homemade burgers, so write the recipe for your favourite chicken, lamb, pork or beef burgers on a card to give with this gift.

2 tablespoons vegetable oil

2 cloves garlic, crushed

1 small fresh red chilli, chopped finely

1 tablespoon yellow mustard seeds

2 medium (300g) brown onions, chopped

2 medium (400g) red capsicums, chopped

2 medium (400g) green capsicums, chopped

2kg peaches, peeled, chopped

2 cups (500ml) white vinegar

1 cup (200g) firmly packed brown sugar

Heat oil in large pan, add garlic, chilli, seeds and onion, cook, stirring, 1 minute.

Add capsicum, cook, stirring, 1 minute. Add peaches, vinegar and sugar, stir constantly, over low heat, without boiling, until sugar dissolves. Bring to boil, simmer, uncovered, 45 minutes or until relish is thick, stirring occasionally.

Pour relish into hot sterilised jars; seal immediately.

Best made 1 week ahead
Storage refrigerator, up to 3 months

recycling

You don't have to spend a lot of money on the wrappings for homemade gifts from the kitchen: recycled jars and bottles, bamboo boxes, even fabrics such as hessian, are ideal. When filling jars and bottles, make sure they are sterilised (rinse cycle/high temperature with no detergent in dishwasher; or boil for 20 minutes in pan).

turkish delight

For presentation, line an acetate box with richly coloured paper and tie with gold organza ribbon.

4 cups (880g) caster sugar

1 litre (4 cups) water

1 teaspoon lemon juice

1 cup (150g) cornflour

1 teaspoon cream of tartar

1½ tablespoons rosewater

red food-colouring

½ cup (80g) chopped, toasted almond kernels, skin on (optional)

1 cup (160g) icing sugar mixture

Combine caster sugar, 1½ cups of the water and the juice in medium pan. Stir over low heat, without boiling, until sugar dissolves. Brush sugar crystals from side of pan with brush dipped in water. Simmer, uncovered, without stirring, until temperature reaches 116°C on candy thermometer (a teaspoon of mixture will form a soft ball when dropped into a glass of cold water). Remove from heat.

Meanwhile, in separate medium pan, blend cornflour and cream of tartar with enough of the remaining water to make a smooth paste. Stir in remaining water, whisk constantly over heat until mixture boils and thickens.

Gradually pour hot syrup, in a thin stream, into cornflour mixture, whisking constantly. Simmer gently, uncovered, about 1 hour or until mixture is translucent and pale straw colour; stir occasionally during cooking.

Stir in rosewater and tint with food-colouring. Mix in toasted almonds, if using. Pour and spread into greased deep 19cm square cake pan, stand, uncovered, 3 hours or overnight.

Cut jelly into squares with an oiled knife. Coat squares in sifted icing sugar mixture.

Best made 1 day ahead
Storage airtight container, up to 1 month

32 honey bubble slice

Cut slice into finger lengths before packing in a special gift box. It's easy to make and children love to help.

200g butter, chopped

1/3 cup (80ml) honey

3/4 cup (75g) instant malted milk powder

2 cups (70g) Rice Bubbles

2 cups (60g) Corn Flakes

1 cup (100g) plain cake crumbs

1/2 cup (45g) desiccated coconut

1/2 cup (40g) flaked almonds, toasted

Best made 1 day ahead
Storage refrigerate, covered, up to 1 week

Grease 20 x 30cm lamington pan, cover base and 2 sides with baking paper, extending paper 2cm above edge of pan.
Place butter, honey and malted milk powder in large pan. Stir over heat until butter is melted. Stir in Rice Bubbles, Corn Flakes, crumbs, coconut and almonds; mix well. Press mixture over base of prepared pan. Cover, refrigerate until firm.

white chocolate fudge 33

Change the colour of the sugar crystals and the shape of the cutter to suit the occasion. Try red hearts for Valentine's Day, blue dolphins for young children or red and green canes for Christmas. Or omit the sugar crystals altogether, and cut fudge into small pieces. Children love to help and this recipe is easy enough for them to make with only a little guidance.

200g white marshmallows

60g butter

2 tablespoons water

400g white chocolate, chopped

coloured sugar crystals

sweets to decorate

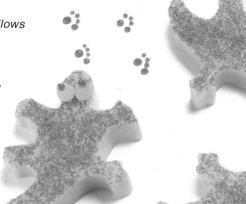

Lightly grease 19cm square cake pan, cover base and 2 sides with baking paper, extending paper 2cm above edge of pan.

Place marshmallows, butter and water in small pan. Stir over low heat, without boiling, until marshmallows are melted. Add chocolate, stir over low heat until smooth (the mixture will become thick). Pour mixture into prepared pan; sprinkle top with coloured sugar crystals; pat down lightly.

Cover, refrigerate until firm. Remove from pan; cut into desired shapes; decorate with sweets.

Makes about 8, depending on size and shape of cutter
Best made 1 day ahead
Storage undecorated, refrigerate, covered, up to 1 week; decorated, refrigerate, covered, up to 2 days

34 a trio of truffles

Package these truffles together or separately as a lovely gift for a chocoholic friend.

fruity coffee liqueur truffles

1/3 cup (80ml) cream
1 2/3 cups (250g) white chocolate Melts, chopped
1/3 cup (50g) dried currants
1 1/2 tablespoons Kahlua or Tia Maria
1 cup (100g) plain cake crumbs
2 tablespoons finely chopped glace figs
3/4 cup (65g) desiccated coconut, approximately

Heat cream in small pan until boiling; pour over chocolate Melts in medium heatproof bowl, stir until smooth. Stir in currants, liqueur, crumbs and figs. Cover, refrigerate until firm.

Roll rounded teaspoons of mixture into balls, roll in coconut; refrigerate until required.

Makes about 45, each recipe
Best made 1 day ahead
Storage refrigerate, covered, up to 2 weeks

rich amaretti truffles

250g dark chocolate, chopped
30g butter
1/3 cup (80ml) cream
2 tablespoons Creme de Cacao
1 tablespoon finely chopped glace ginger
9 (60g) amaretti macaroons, crushed finely
1/2 cup (50g) cocoa powder

Combine chocolate, butter and cream in medium heatproof bowl over pan of simmering water; stir until smooth. Remove from heat. Stir in liqueur, ginger and macaroon crumbs; cool. Cover, refrigerate until firm.

Roll rounded teaspoons of mixture into balls; drop into a bowl of sifted cocoa, toss to coat. Cover, refrigerate until required. Just before giving, shake away excess cocoa.

macadamia truffles

250g milk chocolate, chopped
30g butter
1/3 cup (80ml) cream
1 1/2 tablespoons dark rum
1 1/2 cups (150g) chocolate cake crumbs
1/2 cup (75g) unsalted macadamia halves, toasted
1 2/3 cups (250g) milk chocolate Melts
50g Copha, chopped

Combine chocolate, butter and cream in medium heatproof bowl over pan of simmering water; stir until smooth. Remove from heat, stir in rum, cake crumbs and nuts. Cover, refrigerate until firm.

Roll teaspoons of mixture into balls, refrigerate until firm.

Melt chocolate Melts and Copha in small heatproof bowl over pan of simmering water; stir until smooth. Dip balls into chocolate mixture, place on baking-paper covered trays; refrigerate until set.

sweet orange
marmalade

English muffins or homemade scones would make the perfect partner for this marmalade.

1kg oranges
1.25 litres (5 cups) water
2 teaspoons citric acid
2 tablespoons lemon juice
5 cups (1.5kg) sugar

Cut oranges into quarters. Using a sharp knife, remove pith and rind from each quarter, reserve half the pith. Cut orange flesh into thin slices, place in a bowl; reserve seeds. Cut rind into very thin strips, place in bowl with orange flesh, add half the water, cover, stand overnight.
Tie reserved seeds and pith in piece of muslin, place bag in separate bowl with citric acid and remaining water; cover, stand overnight.
Transfer contents of bowls with lemon juice to large pan, bring to boil, simmer, covered, about 40 minutes or until rind is soft. Discard muslin bag.
Add sugar, stir over heat, without boiling, until sugar is dissolved. Bring to boil, boil, uncovered, without stirring, about 15 minutes or until marmalade jells when a spoonful is placed on a cold saucer. Pour into hot sterilised jars; seal immediately.

Makes about 1.25 litres (5 cups)
Best made 1 day ahead
Storage cool, dark place, up to 1 year.
Refrigerate once opened

grapefruit

marmalade

Store in decorative jars and when you are ready to give the marmalade away, attach a small spoon to the rim using ribbon or raffia, and you have an instant gift.

1kg grapefruit

2 medium (360g) lemons

2.5 litres (10 cups) water

10 cups (2.5 kg) sugar, approximately

Cut unpeeled fruit in half, slice halves thinly, discard seeds. Combine fruit and water in large bowl, cover; stand overnight.

Transfer mixture to large pan, bring to boil, simmer, covered, about 45 minutes or until rind is soft.

Measure fruit mixture, allow 1 cup (220g) sugar to each cup of fruit mixture. Return fruit mixture and sugar to pan, stir over heat until sugar is dissolved.

Boil, uncovered, without stirring, for about 15 minutes or until marmalade jells when tested on a cold saucer. Pour into hot sterilised jars; seal immediately.

Makes about 10 cups

Best made 1 day ahead

Storage cool dark place, up to 1 year. Refrigerate once opened

valentine butter
biscuits

These are also a charming Mother's Day present. Change the shape of the biscuits and the colour of the icing to suit the occasion. Try green iced Christmas trees, yellow iced stars and red iced bells for Christmas.

1¼ cups (185g) plain flour
¾ cup (90g) almond meal
125g butter, chopped
⅓ cup (55g) icing sugar mixture
1 egg
1 tablespoon milk

Process flour, almond meal, butter, icing sugar, egg and milk until mixture forms a ball. Knead dough on floured surface until smooth, cover; refrigerate 30 minutes.
Roll dough between sheets of baking paper until 4mm thick. Cut shapes from dough using heart-shaped cookie cutter. Place on greased oven trays, 3cm apart.
Bake in moderate oven about 8 minutes, or until firm. Stand biscuits 5 minutes; transfer to wire racks. Spread biscuits with Royal Icing when cold.
Royal Icing Beat one egg white in small bowl with electric mixer until just frothy; gradually beat in enough sifted icing sugar (about 1½ cups/240g) for mixture to form stiff peaks. Tint half the mixture a delicate pink with red food colouring and leave remainder white. Keep the icing covered with a damp tea-towel to prevent it from drying out.

VARIATIONS
Jam Centres When biscuits are on oven trays, but before they are baked, using a floured, round wooden spoon handle, make a small indentation in the centre of biscuits. Fill indentations with about ¼ teaspoon of jam of your choice, then bake as above.
Almond When biscuits are on trays, but before they are baked, brush tops lightly with beaten egg, leaving a 1cm border. Top with slivered or flaked almonds, then bake as above.
Sugared When biscuits are on trays, but before they are baked, place a small amount of caster sugar in a plastic bag, tint with pink food-colouring; shake well. Brush tops of biscuits with lightly beaten egg, leaving a 1cm border. Sprinkle coloured sugar over egg, then bake as above.

Makes about 40
Best made 1 day ahead
Storage airtight container, up to 1 week

40 chocolate
orange sticks

Wrap these in cellophane and give in small quantities as after-dinner treats.

2 large (600g) thick-skinned oranges
1 cup (250ml) water
1 cup (220g) caster sugar
125g dark chocolate

Quarter oranges, peel away skin, including white pith. Cut skin into strips 1cm wide.
Drop strips of skin into medium pan of boiling water, return to boil; drain. Repeat boiling and draining twice more.
Combine water and sugar in medium pan, stir over heat, without boiling, until sugar is dissolved. Add orange strips, bring to boil, simmer, uncovered, 7 minutes or until strips become translucent. Stir gently from time to time while simmering.
Using 2 forks or tongs, remove orange strips from pan to wire rack over tray. Allow to dry overnight.
Melt chocolate in small heatproof bowl over simmering water. Dip half of each orange strip into chocolate, place on tray covered with foil. Stand, uncovered, at room temperature until set.

Makes about 70
Best made 1 day ahead
Storage refrigerate, covered, up to 1 week

double
chocolate bites

These are rich, so make small parcels of them for gifts.

200g white marshmallows
60g butter
125g white chocolate, chopped
1¹/₂ cups (285g) dark Choc Bits, melted

Grease an 8 x 26cm bar pan, line base with foil; grease foil.
Combine marshmallows and butter in medium pan, stir over low heat until marshmallows are melted; do not boil. Remove pan from heat.
Add white chocolate, stir until smooth. Beat for 1 minute with wooden spoon. Spread mixture into prepared pan, cover, refrigerate 3 hours or until set.
Remove mixture from pan, cut into 2cm cubes. Dip cubes in melted chocolate. Place on foil-covered tray, drizzle with any remaining chocolate, refrigerate until firm.

Makes about 50
Best made 1 day ahead
Storage refrigerate, covered, for up to 2 weeks

42 lime and poppyseed
buttons

Place these in a small box lined with lime-green paper to give a sneak preview of the flavour within. Try lemons or oranges instead of limes.

200g butter, chopped

3/4 cup (165g) caster sugar

1 teaspoon finely grated lime rind

1 egg

13/4 cups (160g) plain flour

2 teaspoons poppy-seeds

lime icing

1/2 cup (80g) icing sugar mixture

1 tablespoon lime juice

Beat butter, sugar, rind and egg in medium bowl with electric mixer until pale. Gradually beat in flour, then seeds. Cover; refrigerate 30 minutes.
Roll level teaspoons of mixture into balls, place on baking paper-lined oven trays; flatten slightly with fingers. Bake in moderate oven about 8 minutes; leave to stand on tray 5 minutes before transferring to wire rack to cool. Drizzle with Lime Icing; allow to set. Dust with sifted icing sugar if desired.
Lime Icing Place icing sugar into small bowl, gradually stir in lime juice.

Makes about 100
Storage airtight container up to 2 weeks; un-iced biscuits can be frozen for up to 2 months

coconut

crunch cookies

Simple to make, take these to a friend's place when you're invited to tea.

200g butter

1 cup (220g) caster sugar

1 egg

1 teaspoon vanilla essence

1 cup (150g) self-raising flour

1 cup (90g) desiccated coconut, toasted

Makes about 60
Best made 1 day ahead
Storage cooked biscuits: airtight container up to 1 week; uncooked dough: refrigerate up to 1 week or freeze up to 2 months

Beat butter, sugar, egg and essence in bowl with electric mixer until pale and fluffy. Beat in flour and coconut. Cover, refrigerate 1 hour.
Divide dough in half. Place each half onto plastic wrap and shape into a 22cm long roll. Place on a tray and refrigerate overnight.
Cut dough into 5mm thick slices. Place on baking paper-lined oven trays about 5cm apart, bake in moderate oven about 8 minutes. Stand cookies on trays 5 minutes before cooling on wire racks. Dust lightly with sifted icing sugar, if desired.

honey oven-baked
muesli

Put muesli in an attractive jar and give it to a young person in their first flat, along with a brightly coloured cereal bowl and a spoon to match.

1/2 cup (45g) dried apple
1/2 cup (85g) dried dates
3/4 cup (135g) dried pawpaw
3/4 cup (135g) dried pineapple
1/2 cup (85g) raisins
1 cup (40g) flaked coconut
2 tablespoons sunflower seed kernels
2 tablespoons sesame seeds
2 cups (185g) rolled oats

1 cup (100g) rolled triticale
1 cup (50g) wholegrain rye flakes
1 cup (60g) unprocessed oat bran
1/2 cup (30g) unprocessed rice bran
1/3 cup (55g) pepitas
1 cup (155g) pecans
1/2 cup (125ml) vegetable oil
1/2 cup (125ml) honey
2 tablespoons whole linseeds
1 tablespoon lecithin granules

Chop dried fruit, combine in bowl; reserve.
Combine coconut, sunflower seeds, sesame seeds, oats, triticale, rye flakes, oat and rice bran, pepitas and pecans in large baking dish. Pour combined oil and honey over ingredients in dish; stir to coat all ingredients. Cook, uncovered, in moderate oven 20 minutes or until muesli is lightly toasted, stirring every 5 minutes; cool.
Stir fruit, linseeds and lecithin into muesli. Store in airtight container.

Makes about 12 1/2 cups
Best made 1 day ahead
Storage airtight container, in refrigerator, up to 3 months

fudge-topped
brownies

Cut into small squares and dust tops of brownies with alternating stripes of cocoa and icing sugar mixture just before wrapping.

Grease 23cm square slab pan, line base and 2 sides with baking paper, extending paper 2cm above edges of pan.

Melt butter in medium pan, stir in chocolate. Stir over low heat until smooth. Transfer to large bowl. Stir in sugar and eggs. Stir in sifted flours and cocoa until combined. Spread mixture into prepared pan. Bake in moderate oven about 35 minutes. Cool in pan. Top brownie with White Chocolate Fudge, cover, refrigerate until firm.

White Chocolate Fudge Melt butter in medium pan over low heat. Stir in chocolate, condensed milk and liqueur. Stir over heat until smooth.

125g unsalted butter

2 cups (300g) dark chocolate Melts

1¹/₂ cups (330g) caster sugar

3 eggs, beaten lightly

³/₄ cup (110g) plain flour

¹/₄ cup (35g) self-raising flour

¹/₃ cup (35g) cocoa powder

white chocolate fudge

60g unsalted butter

2¹/₂ cups (375g) white chocolate Melts, chopped finely

400g can sweetened condensed milk

1 tablespoon Amaretto

Best made 1 day ahead
Storage refrigerate, covered, up to 1 week

macadamia maple
nougat

As the sides of the nougat are very sticky it is best to line the container with edible rice paper before placing the nougat in it.

three 15 x 23cm rice paper sheets

2 cups (440g) sugar

1 cup (250ml) glucose syrup

1/2 cup (125ml) maple syrup

1 teaspoon vanilla essence

2 egg whites

75g butter, softened

1 1/2 cups (225g) macadamias, toasted

Grease 19 x 29cm rectangular slice pan. Line base with 1 1/2 sheets of rice paper.

Combine sugar, syrups and essence in medium heavy-based pan, stir over heat, without boiling, until sugar dissolves. Boil, uncovered, without stirring, about 6 minutes, or until mixture reaches 138°C on candy thermometer (small crack stage – a teaspoon of mixture will snap when dropped into a cup of cold water).

Meanwhile beat egg whites in small bowl with electric mixer until firm peaks form; transfer to large bowl. With mixer operating, gradually pour in hot syrup in a thin stream. Beat about 3 minutes or until mixture holds its shape. Add butter, beat until combined, stir in nuts.

Spread mixture immediately into prepared pan, smooth top. Press remaining rice paper on nougat.

Cool to room temperature, remove from pan. Using an oiled knife, cut into 3cm squares.

Makes about 54
Best made 1 day ahead
Storage airtight container in cool dry place, up to 2 weeks

48 panforte
di sienna

Place the panforte in a lined cake tin and dust with sifted icing sugar.

2 sheets 15 x 23cm rice paper

3/4 cup (125g) brazil nuts, toasted

1/2 cup (80g) blanched almonds, toasted

1/2 cup (95g) chopped dried figs

1/2 cup (125g) chopped glacé apricots

1/4 cup (50g) glacé ginger, chopped finely

1/3 cup (55g) chopped raisins

2 tablespoons cocoa powder

1/4 cup (35g) plain flour

1/2 teaspoon ground nutmeg

1/2 teaspoon ground coriander

1/4 teaspoon ground cloves

1/4 cup (60ml) honey

1/4 cup (55g) caster sugar

1 tablespoon water

Grease deep 17cm round cake pan, line base and side with baking paper, then cover base with rice paper.

Combine nuts, fruit, sifted cocoa, flour and spices in bowl. Combine honey, sugar and water in small heavy-based pan, stir over heat until sugar dissolves, then boil, uncovered, without stirring, about 2 minutes or until temperature reaches 116°C on candy thermometer (a teaspoon of mixture will form a soft ball when dropped into a cup of cold water). Mixture must not change colour.

Remove from heat, allow bubbles to subside, pour over nut mixture; mix well. Press mixture into prepared pan. Bake in moderately slow oven about 40 minutes or until cake feels just firm; cool in pan. Remove from pan; wrap in foil; refrigerate overnight.

Best made 1 day ahead
Storage refrigerator, covered, up to 1 week

almond coconut
macaroons

A package of good quality tea and a cellophane bag of macaroons.
Perfection.

2 egg whites

²/₃ cup (150g) caster sugar

1 cup (90g) desiccated coconut

¹/₂ cup shredded coconut

¹/₃ cup (40g) almond meal

2 egg whites, beaten lightly, extra

2 cups (160g) flaked almonds, chopped

Makes about 50
Best made 1 day ahead
Storage airtight container, up to 1 week

In a small bowl, beat egg whites and sugar with electric mixer about 8 minutes or until sugar is dissolved. Stir in coconuts and almond meal; cover, refrigerate overnight.
Roll rounded teaspoons of mixture into 5cm logs, dip into extra egg whites, roll logs in flaked almonds. Place logs about 3cm apart on baking paper-covered oven trays.
Bake in slow oven about 15 minutes or until macaroons are firm; cool on trays.

pistachio

caramel logs

Accompanied by a half bottle of sticky dessert-style wine, Pistachio Caramel Logs make a fine ending to a light dinner.

125g butter, chopped

400g can sweetened condensed milk

2 tablespoons golden syrup

3/4 cup (150g) firmly packed brown sugar

1/2 teaspoon cream of tartar

3/4 cup (110g) shelled pistachios, toasted, chopped finely

Line base and sides of deep 19cm square cake pan with baking paper.

Combine butter, milk, golden syrup, sugar and cream of tartar in medium, heavy-based pan, stir over heat, without boiling, until sugar dissolves. Bring to boil, whisk constantly over heat about 8 minutes or until mixture is thick and dark caramel in colour. Pour mixture into prepared pan. Stand caramel 15 minutes. Mark 6 strips in caramel with a greased knife; cool.

Remove caramel from pan, cut into strips where marked. Roll strips in nuts, shaping each into a 32cm long sausage; press nuts firmly into caramel. Cut diagonally into 4cm pieces.

Makes about 48
Best made 1 day ahead
Storage refrigerate, covered, up to 1 week

biscotti

Deliciously addictive, biscotti are extremely hard. Dunk them in your coffee or a glass of sweet vermouth.

coffee hazelnut biscotti

1 cup (220g) caster sugar
2 eggs
1 1/3 cups (200g) plain flour
1/3 cup (50g) self-raising flour
1 tablespoon espresso-style instant coffee powder
2 teaspoons water
1/3 cup (35g) hazelnut meal
1 cup (150g) roasted hazelnuts

Whisk sugar and eggs together in medium bowl. Stir in flours, combined coffee and water, hazelnut meal and hazelnuts; mix to sticky dough. Divide dough into 2 portions. Using floured hands, roll each portion into a 20cm log, place on lightly greased oven trays. Bake in moderate oven about 35 minutes or until firm; cool on tray.
Cut logs diagonally into 1cm slices, using a serrated knife. Place slices, cut side up, on oven trays. Bake in moderately slow oven about 25 minutes or until crisp and dry, turning once during cooking; cool on trays.
Makes about 30

orange cardamom biscotti

1 cup (220g) caster sugar
2 eggs
2 teaspoons grated orange rind
1 1/3 cups (200g) plain flour
1/3 cup (50g) self-raising flour
2/3 cup (80g) almond meal
1 teaspoon ground cardamom

Whisk sugar, eggs and rind in medium bowl. Stir in flours, almond meal and cardamom; mix to sticky dough. Divide dough into two portions. Using floured hands, roll each portion into a 20cm log, place on greased oven trays. Bake in moderate oven about 35 minutes or until lightly browned; cool on tray.
Cut logs diagonally into 1cm slices, using a serrated knife. Place slices, cut side up, on oven trays. Bake in moderately slow oven about 25 minutes or until dry and crisp, turning once during cooking; cool on trays.
Makes about 30
Best made 2 days ahead, each recipe
Storage airtight container, up to 1 month

Biscotti from top: gingerbread, orange cardamom and coffee hazelnut.

gingerbread biscotti

3 eggs
$3/4$ cup (150g) firmly packed brown sugar
$1/4$ cup (55g) caster sugar
$13/4$ cups (260g) plain flour
$3/4$ cup (110g) self-raising flour
1 tablespoon ground ginger
$11/2$ teaspoons ground cinnamon
$1/2$ teaspoon bicarbonate of soda
$1/2$ teaspoon ground cloves
$1/2$ teaspoon ground nutmeg

Whisk eggs and sugars in small bowl with electric mixer until just changed in colour. Transfer mixture to large bowl.
Stir in sifted dry ingredients; mix to a firm dough. Knead on floured surface until smooth. Divide dough into 2 portions. Using floured hands, roll each portion into 30cm log, place on lightly greased oven trays. Bake in moderate oven 35 minutes or until firm; cool on tray.
Cut logs diagonally into 1cm slices, using a serrated knife. Place slices, cut side up, on oven trays. Bake in moderately slow oven about 15 minutes or until dry and crisp, turning once during cooking; cool on trays.
Makes about 40

coffee and vanilla
twists

Simply wrap in clear cellophane, in bundles, then tie with raffia.

coffee shortbread

1¹/₂ cups (225g) plain flour

60g butter, chopped

1 tablespoon hot milk

2 teaspoons dry instant coffee powder

¹/₄ cup (55g) caster sugar

1 egg, beaten lightly

vanilla shortbread

1¹/₂ cups (225g) plain flour

60g butter, chopped

1 tablespoon milk

¹/₂ cup (55g) caster sugar

1 teaspoon vanilla essence

1 egg, beaten lightly

To make Coffee Shortbread, process flour and butter until combined. Mix together milk, coffee and sugar in small pan, stir over heat until sugar dissolves; cool slightly. With motor operating, gradually add egg, then milk mixture to flour mixture; process until combined. Wrap dough in plastic wrap; refrigerate 1 hour.

To make Vanilla Shortbread, process flour and butter until combined. Mix together milk and sugar in small pan, stir over heat until sugar dissolves; stir in essence. Wtih motor operating, gradually add egg, then milk mixture to flour mixture; process until combined. Wrap dough in plastic wrap; refrigerate 1 hour.

Taking rounded teaspoons of dough at a time, shape Coffee Shortbread dough into thin 15cm-long rolls. Repeat with Vanilla Shortbread dough. Twist a coffee and a vanilla roll together, repeat with remaining rolls. Place twists on lightly greased oven trays. Bake in moderate oven about 15 minutes, or until lightly browned; transfer to wire rack to cool. Dust with sifted cocoa if desired.

Makes about 30
Best made 1 day ahead
Storage airtight container, up to 5 days

palmiers

Give a packet of good-quality cocoa to make beautiful hot chocolate to go with your palmiers.

Roll pastry on surface sprinkled with a little sugar to 20 x 35cm rectangle; trim edges with sharp knife.
Sprinkle pastry lightly with a little more of the sugar. Fold in long sides of rectangle, so they meet in the centre, sprinkle with a little more sugar, fold in half lengthways, press lightly; cover, refrigerate 30 minutes.
Cut pastry roll into 12mm slices, place about 10cm apart onto lightly greased oven trays. Bake in moderately hot oven 10 minutes, turn palmiers with egg slide, bake further 10 minutes or until crisp and browned.
Lift onto wire racks to cool. Lightly dust with sifted icing sugar if desired.

375g packet frozen puff pastry, thawed

2 tablespoons caster sugar, approximately

Makes about 25
Best made 1 day ahead
Storage airtight container, up to 1 week

honey-drenched
anise slice

Some Turkish or Greek-style coffee with a jar of cardamom pods to make the coffee taste great is all you need to finish off this gift.

2 cups (300g) self-raising flour

1 cup (150g) plain flour

3 teaspoons anise seeds

1 teaspoon ground cinnamon

1/2 cup (80g) fine semolina

1/2 cup (110g) caster sugar

1/2 cup (70g) slivered almonds, toasted

3/4 cup (180ml) vegetable oil

1/2 cup (125ml) milk

1 egg, beaten lightly

1 tablespoon honey

honey syrup

1 1/2 cups (375ml) honey

1/3 cup (80ml) water

1/3 cup (75g) caster sugar

Grease 20 x 30cm lamington pan. Sift flours into large bowl; add remaining ingredients; stir until a soft dough forms. Press over base of prepared pan. Bake in moderate oven about 30 minutes.

Pour hot Honey Syrup over hot slice; cool in pan, before cutting.

Honey Syrup Combine all ingredients in medium pan, stir over heat, without boiling, until sugar dissolves. Simmer, uncovered, without stirring, 2 minutes.

Best made 1 day ahead
Storage airtight container, up to 1 week

peanut brittle

Although it is dangerous for children to make peanut brittle because of the hot toffee, they will love to give it to friends for a special occasion. Break it into big chunks and place in clear boxes.

Spread nuts onto a greased oven tray; place tray on a wooden board.
Combine sugars, syrup and water in medium heavy-based pan, stir over low heat, without boiling, until sugar dissolves.
Add butter, boil, uncovered, without stirring, until temperature reaches 150°C on candy thermometer (crack stage – 1 teaspoon of mixture will snap when dropped into a cup of cold water).
Remove from heat, allow bubbles to subside, quickly stir in soda, pour evenly over nuts; do not scrape mixture from pan. Stand at room temperature to set. Break into pieces.

2¹/₂ cups (375g) unsalted roasted peanuts

³/₄ cup (165g) caster sugar

1 cup (200g) firmly packed brown sugar

¹/₂ cup (125ml) golden syrup

1 cup (250ml) water

60g butter

¹/₄ teaspoon bicarbonate of soda

Best made 1 day ahead
Storage airtight container in cool, dry place, up to 1 week

apricot almond **bread**

Wrap the Apricot Almond Bread in small bundles using pale green rice paper and gold ribbon, it will be sure to delight any recipient.

2 egg whites

1/3 cup (75g) caster sugar

3/4 cup (110g) plain flour

1/4 teaspoon ground cinnamon

1/4 teaspoon ground nutmeg

1/4 teaspoon ground ginger

1/3 cup (55g) almond kernels, skin on

1/3 cup (50g) shelled pistachios

1/2 cup (75g) chopped dried apricots

Grease or oil an 8 x 26cm bar pan, line base and sides with baking paper.

Beat egg whites and sugar in a small bowl with electric mixer about 8 minutes or until sugar dissolves.

Fold in sifted dry ingredients, nuts and apricots; spread into prepared pan.

Bake in moderate oven about 30 minutes or until lightly browned. Cool in pan, wrap in foil; stand overnight.

Using a serrated knife, slice bread very thinly. Place slices on baking paper-covered oven trays, bake in slow oven about 20 minutes or until dry and crisp.

Makes about 70
Best made 1 day ahead
Storage airtight container, up to 2 weeks

glossary

almond meal also known as ground almonds.

amaretti macaroons small Italian-style biscuits based on almond meal.

anise seeds a licorice-flavoured seed.

bay leaves aromatic leaves from the bay tree.

bicarbonate of soda also known as baking soda.

blacan also known as belacan, dried shrimp paste sold in slabs or flat cakes.

candlenut a hard nut, used to thicken curries in Malaysia and Indonesia. Almonds, brazil nuts or macadamias can be substituted.

capers pickled buds of a Mediterranean shrub. The smaller the better.

caraway seeds a member of the parsley family, it is available in seed or ground form and can be used in sweet and savoury dishes.

cardamom an expensive spice with a sweet, exotic fragrance. It can be bought in pods, as seed or in ground form.

chilli available in many different types and sizes, used fresh and dried. Rubber gloves should be used when seeding and chopping chillies (both fresh and dried) to avoid burning your skin. Removing seeds and membranes decreases the heat level.

choc bits also known as chocolate chips and chocolate morsels; available in milk, white and dark chocolate. Made of cocoa liquor, cocoa butter, sugar and emulsifier, these hold their shape in baking and are ideal for decorating.

chocolate melts for melting and moulding.

citric acid commonly found in most fruits, especially limes and lemons. Commercial citric acid helps to accentuate the acid flavour of fruit; it does not act as a preservative.

copha a solid white shortening based on coconut oil. Often used with melted chocolate.

cream of tartar an ingredient in baking powder. It is also sometimes added to confectionery mixtures to help prevent sugar from crystallising.

fenugreek seeds hard, dried seed usually sold ground as an astringent spice powder. Good with seafood and in chutneys, fenugreek helps mask unpleasant odours.

fetta cheese Greek in origin; a crumbly-textured goat's or sheep's milk cheese, having a sharp, salty taste.

food colouring available in liquid, powdered and concentrated paste forms.

garam masala a blend of spices, originating in North India; based on varying proportions of cardamom, cinnamon, cloves, coriander, fennel and cumin, roasted and ground together. Black pepper and chilli can be added, to make a hotter example.

ginger, fresh also called root ginger.

glucose syrup also called liquid glucose, made from wheat starch.

golden syrup maple syrup or honey can be substituted. Do not use the golden syrup available in squeeze bottles as results will vary.

hazelnut meal also known as ground hazelnuts

icing sugar mixture icing sugar with the addition of cornflour.

juniper berries dried berries of an evergreen tree, it is the main flavouring ingredient of gin.

lecithin granules available in health food shops

lemon grass a tall, clumping, lemon-smelling and tasting grass, the white lower part of stem is used in Asian cooking.

macadamia nut rich and buttery, store in refrigerator because of high fat content.

mustard seeds can be black or yellow.

pepitas dried pumpkin seeds.

pine nuts also called pignoli; small, cream-coloured kernels obtained from the cones of different varieties of pine trees.

pistachio pale green, delicately flavoured nut inside hard off-white shells.

poppyseeds tiny black seeds with a pungent flavour; store in an airtight container in a cool place or freeze, as they can become rancid.

rice paper an edible paper used as a wrapper or to line pans; available from specialty food shops and Asian suppliers.

rosewater extract made from crushed rose petals, called gulab in India; used for its aromatic quality in many sweetmeats and desserts.

rum, dark we prefer to use an underproof rum (not overproof), for a more subtle flavour.

semolina made from durum wheat milled into various textured granules.

sesame oil made from roasted, crushed white sesame seeds. Do not use for frying.

sesame seeds to toast, spread seeds evenly onto oven tray, toast in moderate oven for about 5 minutes.

shrimp paste a powerful dark brown flavouring made from salted dried shrimp.

sunflower seed kernels from dried husked sunflower seeds.

vermouth a wine flavoured with a number of different herbs, mostly used as an aperitif and for cocktails.

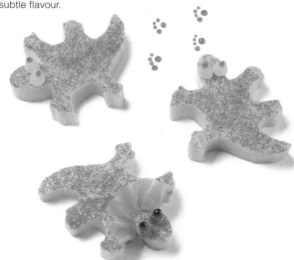

index

These conversions are approximate only, but the difference between an exact and the approximate conversion of various liquid and dry measures is minimal and will not affect your cooking results.

Measuring equipment

The difference between one country's measuring cups and another's is, at most, within a 2 or 3 teaspoon variance. (For the record, 1 Australian metric measuring cup holds approximately 250ml.) The most accurate way of measuring dry ingredients is to weigh them. For liquids, use a clear glass or plastic jug having metric markings.

Note: NZ, Canada, USA and UK all use 15ml tablespoons. Australian tablespoons measure 20ml.
All cup and spoon measurements are level.

How to measure

When using graduated measuring cups, shake dry ingredients loosely into the appropriate cup. Do not tap the cup on a bench or tightly pack the ingredients unless directed to do so. Level the top of measuring cups and measuring spoons with a knife. When measuring liquids, place a clear glass or plastic jug having metric markings on a flat surface to check accuracy at eye level.

Dry Measures

metric	imperial
15g	1/2oz
30g	1oz
60g	2oz
90g	3oz
125g	4oz (1/4lb)
155g	5oz
185g	6oz
220g	7oz
250g	8oz (1/2lb)
280g	9oz
315g	10oz
345g	11oz
375g	12oz (3/4lb)
410g	13oz
440g	14oz
470g	15oz
500g	16oz (1lb)
750g	24oz (1 1/2lb)
1kg	32oz (2lb)

We use large eggs having an average weight of 60g.

Liquid Measures

metric	imperial
30ml	1 fluid oz
60ml	2 fluid oz
100ml	3 fluid oz
125ml	4 fluid oz
150ml	5 fluid oz (1/4 pint/1 gill)
190ml	6 fluid oz
250ml (1cup)	8 fluid oz
300ml	10 fluid oz (1/2 pint)
500ml	16 fluid oz
600ml	20 fluid oz (1 pint)
1000ml (1litre)	1 3/4 pints

Helpful Measures

metric	imperial
3mm	1/8in
6mm	1/4in
1cm	1/2in
2cm	3/4in
2.5cm	1in
6cm	2 1/2in
8cm	3in
20cm	8in
23cm	9in
25cm	10in
30cm	12in (1ft)

Oven Temperatures

These oven temperatures are only a guide.
Always check the manufacturer's manual.

	C°(Celsius)	F°(Fahrenheit)	Gas Mark
Very slow	120	250	1
Slow	150	300	2
Moderately slow	160	325	3
Moderate	180 –190	350 – 375	4
Moderately hot	200 – 210	400 – 425	5
Hot	220 – 230	450 – 475	6
Very hot	240 – 250	500 – 525	7

Food editor Pamela Clark
Associate food editor Karen Hammial
Assistant food editor Kathy McGarry
Recipe editor Karen Green
Assistant recipe editor Elizabeth Hooper

HOME LIBRARY STAFF
Editor-in-chief Mary Coleman
Marketing manager Nicole Pizanis
Editor Susan Tomnay
Concept design Jackie Richards
Designer Jackie Richards
Group publisher Paul Dykzeul
Chief executive officer John Alexander

Produced by *The Australian Women's Weekly*
Home Library, Sydney.

Colour separations by
ACP Colour Graphics Pty Ltd, Sydney.
Printing by Diamond Press Limited, Sydney.

Published by ACP Publishing Pty Limited,
54 Park St, Sydney; GPO Box 4088, Sydney,
NSW 1028. Ph: (02) 9282 8618
Fax: (02) 9267 9438.

AWWHomeLib@publishing.acp.com.au

Australia Distributed by Network Distribution
Company, GPO Box 4088, Sydney, NSW 1028.
Ph: (02) 9282 8777 Fax: (02) 9264 3278.

United Kingdom Distributed by Australian
Consolidated Press (UK), Moulton Park
Business Centre, Red House Rd, Moulton Park,
Northampton, NN3 6AQ. Ph: (01604) 497 531
Fax: (01604) 497 533 Acpukltd@aol.com

Canada Distributed by Whitecap Books Ltd,
351 Lynn Ave, North Vancouver, BC, V7J 2C4,
(604) 980 9852.

New Zealand Distributed by Netlink Distribution
Company, 17B Hargreaves St,
Level 5, College Hill, Auckland 1, (9) 302 7616.

South Africa Distributed by PSD Promotions
(Pty) Ltd,PO Box 1175, Isando 1600, SA,
(011) 392 6065.

Creative Food: Gourmet Gifts

Includes index.
ISBN 1 86396 149 6.

1 Cookery. 2. Gifts. I Title: Australian Women's
Weekly. (Series: Australian Women's Weekly
creative food mini series).
641.514

© ACP Publishing Pty Limited 1999
ACN 053 273 546

Cover Coconut crunch cookies, page 43.
Stylist Michelle Noerianto
Photographer Brett Danton
Back cover Panforte di sienna, page 48

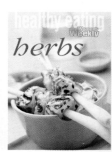

In the series

- healthy eating
- make it tonight
- sweet and simple
- creative food